Freedom.

You can handle it...

But hurry!

Second Edition

Gary Henderson

Cover design by Gary Henderson
Cover photographs by MBPhoto, Inc via iStockPhoto.
Used by permission.

ISBN 978-1-937975-01-2
Second edition, print format

Electronic book version available as ISBN 978-1-937975-02-9

RNWC Media, LLC
PO Box 559
Pinehurst, TX 77362

www.RNWCMedia.com
www.Freedom-YouCanHandleIt.com
www.FreedomTheBook.com

Dedicated to the founders, who risked everything to give us freedom, and to those who fight today to preserve that freedom for our children and those yet to come.

Special thanks to those who have contributed so much to explain how America began, to clarify the American ideals, and to promote liberty and Constitutional restoration, including among many others Dr. Walter E. Williams, Mark Alexander and the Patriot Post, Dr. Larry Arnn and Hillsdale College, Dr. Edwin Feulner and The Heritage Foundation, Mark Levin and the Landmark Legal Foundation, Michael Boldin and the Tenth Amendment Center, Sheriff Richard Mack and the Constitutional Sheriffs and Peace Officers Association, and those who are speaking, writing, broadcasting, running for office, and serving as elected officials around the nation.

Together we can preserve that which we must not lose.

WHAT PEOPLE ARE SAYING ABOUT THE FIRST EDITION

"Obviously, Gary Henderson knows and understands the only solution remaining if we are to restore America to her original purpose. In this new and fantastic book, 'Freedom. You Can Handle It. But Hurry!' Henderson explains the solution directly and succinctly. Now it's up to us! I hope we hurry!"

Sheriff Richard Mack
www.SheriffMack.com and www.CSPOA.org
Author of "The County Sheriff: America's Last Hope"
and "The Victory for State Sovereignty: Mack/Printz v. USA"

"Freedom! You Can Handle It! But Hurry!" is an outstanding contribution to the effort to advance the message of Liberty to Grassroots Patriots, especially those new to our shores from other nations!"

Mark Alexander
Publisher, The Patriot Post
www.PatriotPost.us
Pro Deo et Constitutione -- Libertas aut Mors
Semper Vigilo, Fortis, Paratus et Fidelis

TABLE OF CONTENTS

FROM THE DECLARATION OF INDEPENDENCE

We hold these truths to be self-evident, that all men are created equal, that they are endowed by their Creator with certain unalienable Rights, that among these are Life, Liberty and the pursuit of Happiness.

That to secure these rights, Governments are instituted among Men, deriving their just powers from the consent of the governed, That whenever any Form of Government becomes destructive of these ends, it is the Right of the People to alter or to abolish it, and to institute new Government, laying its foundation on such principles and organizing its powers in such form, as to them shall seem most likely to effect their Safety and Happiness.

Prudence, indeed, will dictate that Governments long established should not be changed for light and transient causes; and accordingly all experience hath shewn, that mankind are more disposed to suffer, while evils are sufferable, than to right themselves by abolishing the forms to which they are accustomed.

But when a long train of abuses and usurpations, pursuing invariably the same Object evinces a design to reduce them under absolute Despotism, it is their right, it is their duty, to throw off such Government, and to provide new Guards for their future security.

You can read the entire Declaration, the Constitution, and many other important documents at The Patriot Post:

http://patriotpost.us/document/

Freedom.

You can handle it.

But hurry!

INTRODUCTION

Freedom is never more than one generation away from extinction, said President Reagan. You are that generation.

The Republic they gave us almost 250 years ago is collapsing. We have forgotten how to be free. But it's not too late.

Freedom! You can handle it. But you need to hurry.

War is easy, by comparison. You attack, you defend. Life or death, and soon it is over.

Freedom is harder. Most people never have it, and those who do are under constant attack, suddenly waking up in the chains of slavery they did not see coming upon them.

America is about to wake up in chains. We created a central government to do a few simple things for us. Like an ugly cancer, it has metastasized into an all-consuming, grotesque distortion of its original form. We created a servant, but it has become a monster. The Transformer has gone bad. It has escaped the factory where we built it, and is terrorizing the country.

No matter who gets elected, the central government continues to grow. Some leaders slow the growth down, others accelerate it, but still the government grows. Every small growth of government is at your expense — you lose choices, you lose money, you lose freedom, and your children lose their future.

This is important. As John Adams wrote to his wife, "Liberty, once lost, is lost forever."

Here's an example of how hard it is to stop this cancerous growth. One measure of the size of government is how much of your money they are spending. In the spring of 2011, Congress fought over how to reduce the country's budget; after a huge effort, here's the result: for every $1400 they were spending, they would now only spend $1,399.

Are you impressed?

So, already fourteen trillion dollars in debt at that time – that's a "14" with twelve zeros after it!– they needed to borrow another trillion and a half, just to keep going. And it's much worse now.

It's hard to realize how bad this is. The numbers are just too big. At that time they needed to repay $14,000,000,000,000, plus the interest due on all that money, just to get back to zero, to simply being broke!

Even when we are so deep in debt it's hard to count the zeros on the number, Washington cannot stop borrowing more, spending more, and making it worse. Disaster is coming.

The reason it matters to you is that they think your freedom doesn't matter, that your money is really their money, and they can do whatever they want with both your money and your freedom. If you want to spend your own money, you're being "greedy;" but if they take it, that's good. You're helping. Everyone needs to make a "shared sacrifice," you know, "We're all in this together," and "the rich don't need all that money." So the more they want to spend, the more of your money they take to do it.

This would actually be funny, if it weren't so outrageous and if it weren't doing so much damage.

President Obama once spoke about "expenditures in the tax code." Do you understand? In his mind, all of your money belonged to the government, and if they let you keep any of it, that's an expense, a loss of money for Washington.

There appears to be no end to their arrogance or willingness to take your money and freedom, on the way to bigger government.

What can be done? How can we force the central government back to its rightful functions, restore the freedoms that have been taken away, and ensure that the bright and glorious heritage of America endures for the benefit of our children and the world?

Besides sending the best people we can to Washington, and supporting them in their efforts to somehow get things under control — which has not helped yet — how do we stop the cancerous and illegal growth of the federal government?

The "progressives," who want complete control of your life in order to fix the world's problems, have spent the last 80 years turning our media, our schools, and the Democratic Party into a turbo-charged support system for big government. Is there any solution besides spending the next 80 years trying to undo that damage? Is there anything else we can do?

Yes.

You, and the state you live in, can say, "No." It's that simple.

Here's the deal.

In the beginning, people from each of the states worked together to write the Constitution, which created a central government to do a few specific things, and no more. We did this, you and I. We weren't here yet, but they did it for themselves, for their children, and for us. They said so, and they were standing in for all the rest of us. So we all did it.

Then it went to each of the states that existed then, and when enough of them had signed it, the central government was created.

Did you notice that part about "and no more?" The men who wrote this law were very clear about "and no more." Anything else Washington tries to do, outside of what they were created to do, is simply illegal. In fact, the founders (those who created the Constitution) said that if the new government tried to do anything else, anything more than what we created them to do, it would be an attack on the rights and privileges of the states (that means you and me), and should be resisted or ignored.

Thomas Jefferson, one of our early Presidents and the man who actually drafted the Declaration of Independence, said it is not just the right but the duty of the state you live in to protect you from exactly this danger, this attack of the central government.

So let's get started. We can do it. We can handle freedom, hang onto it, and keep it alive for ourselves, for our children and for their children. We just need to know a few things and then insist that our states stand up for us.

We especially need to understand the authority and freedom that was kept by the states, which means kept for us. These are the things that were NOT given to the central government. Together we can protect those freedoms and put Washington back in its place, if we choose to do so, and if we can do it in time.

There's not much time left. Let's hurry.

Have you ever looked at the Constitution, the supreme law of America? Do you know what it actually says? Many people have strong opinions about what the federal government can and cannot do, but have no idea what's actually in that document. I hope you'll soon understand what was created when America was born and see through the ridiculous excuses that Washington uses to take over so much of our lives today.

If you or your parents came to this country recently in search of freedom and opportunity, please understand that you may soon have neither freedom nor opportunity. Did you see the tyranny of corrupt, powerful leaders in the place you left behind? That's where we're headed. The United States has risen to be the best country — the most free, the most prosperous, the most generous, and the most envied country in the history of the world. Let's keep it that way.

If you went to the public schools in this country recently, you may not have learned much about these ideas. I hope you will be glad to know that the federal government was not created to be your mommy, much less your slave master. You are free to be an adult and run your own life. Let's not lose that!

When we finish, you may understand more of what the fuss was all about in 1776, when this country of free men and women declared itself to the world. You'll know a little more about what it means to be an American. No other country, now or at anytime in history, has had what we have, and we are about to lose it.

FREEDOM. YOU CAN HANDLE IT. BUT HURRY!

THE DREAM

What is that? What are we about to lose?

What do we have that is so special, that no other country has ever had?

We created a country based on the idea that your life, your freedom, and your ability to pursue your own plans and dreams and goals are the most important things.

The job of the government is to protect your rights and that freedom, so you can safely do whatever you want — learn skills, create a business, travel, live where you want, raise a family, teach your children, help your neighbors, follow your dreams, invent things, absolutely whatever you want to do, as long as you respect the rights and freedom of others to do the same.

The job of the government in America is _not_ to control your family, your business, your travel, your education, your healthcare, or your choices of what to eat or drink or say or think or do. None of that is their business.

That's the dream: freedom. That's what they fought for, and delivered into our care. It has never happened like this before. If we lose it, it may never happen again.

Part of the dream is that you are free to follow whatever religion you wish, and that you have the right to the property, the things and places, that you build or acquire by your own honest efforts.

We also believe that about the person next to you.

So you have the responsibility to allow them – the people around you -- that freedom, just as they allow you your freedom. This means you can't do things that wrongly take away their freedom, or their life, or their property, and they can't take away yours.

The role of government is to protect these rights for you; nothing more.

In order to protect those rights for you, government has to have laws and the ability to punish people who harm you. So we elect people to make those laws for us, and we need the courts and the police to enforce them. In order to keep other nations from taking these freedoms from us, we need a strong military.

That's it.

But what's so special about all that?

No other nation on Earth believes it.

Essentially every other country believes that the state or the ruler or the central government is the most important thing, and that you must do what they say. Some countries believe their religion is the most important thing, and will kill people who choose another religion.

We don't. Your freedom is the most important thing, and the only reason to have government is to protect it. That's why people come to America any way they can, and very few by comparison leave America to go live anywhere else.

Now, look around you. Is your government doing everything it can to control you, or everything it can to protect your freedom so you can live your life as you please?

Where does it say this? Where is it written that your freedom is the most important thing, and that the job of the government is to protect your freedom and your rights of life, liberty, and the pursuit of happiness?

The Declaration of Independence, the founding document of this great country. Read it again; it's all there.

A couple of other things are required for this to work.

The government has to be strong, but controlled. The people that make the laws have to be limited to do only what we want, and nothing more – they can only do things with "the consent of the governed" – or they will quickly be trying to control us, making us do what they want instead of what we ourselves choose to do.

To prevent a single person or group from taking control, we have to divide the power: the people who make the laws cannot be the same people who enforce the laws, and neither of those can also be the people who act as judges when we are accused of breaking those laws. This is called "separation of powers."

The core idea behind all of this is that we are in charge, not the government. They work for us. "Sovereignty" is not in Washington, or in the capitol of your state, but in you and me, in the people. Any time we want to do so, we can change the government and do something else, just like they did in 1776.

No other country has that idea built into their system, that requirement that the people must have authority over their "rulers." England used to, but today an Englishman cannot even defend himself against the criminal who breaks into his home. His rulers won't let him.

Why do we want to lose the dream, and become just another bankrupt, broken, corrupt, socialist state ... like all the rest who never had the freedom you have today, or have been careless and let it slip away?

When the central government of a country becomes overwhelmingly strong, bad things happen. In the last hundred years or so governments have killed over 100 million of their own citizens. It has happened everywhere else, and it can happen here as well. Why do you think it won't? We need to get busy.

The Constitution is easy to understand, and you have as much authority to decide what it means as anyone else. We, "the people," created the federal government. They work for us.

We are in charge, but we don't directly run things. We elect people to represent us, so we're not just a mob rushing to fix whatever we're upset about. This gives everyone time to think before acting.

If the government no longer obeys us, we need to fix that problem as soon as we can.

When we let the same people make the law, enforce the law, and be the judges when the law is broken (for example, in the regulatory agencies, like Health, Education, and the EPA), it becomes a nightmare. Congress has betrayed us by allowing agencies that are not accountable to us exercise the authority we gave to Congress, and to them alone.

Men are not angels, as the founders reminded us, so we cannot let any one person or group have such unrestricted power, acting as lawmaker, enforcer, and judge, without accountability to anyone.

The primary purpose of the government is to protect our freedom and rights. It is not to tell us how to live our lives. But keeping it within its proper role requires constant attention and effort, and we have not been paying attention. We're in trouble.

STAND UP. YOU'RE FREE.

It's amazing. We created a strong, permanent society of free men and women, where the government works for the people, protecting their rights instead of controlling them. Name another country in the modern world that has done that! This free society became the most powerful and influential nation on earth. Welcome to America!

Most of the time, in most of the world, people have been at the mercy of their government, often under a king or dictator with the power of life and death over his subjects. But in America, the people are in charge, and we created a central government to do a few things that should be done in a central place — watch the fences, print money, bring us our mail. Sort things out when one state fusses with another. That's about it.

But that was hard. You can't name a country in all the history of this earth that has done it so well. If you haven't learned about George Washington, James Madison, Thomas Jefferson, and the many others who put this country together, you've got a treat coming. Go read about them; they were incredible.

As we mentioned, the central government has to be strong, very strong, to do the hard things that must be done. Taking down terrorists, for example. But it also has to be restrained, held in check, like a strong horse or an ox that could rip its owner apart if it became disobedient or angry.

James Madison said it well: "If men were angels, no government would be necessary. If angels were to govern men, neither external nor internal controls on government would be necessary. In framing a government which is to be administered by men over men, the great difficulty lies in this: you must first enable the government to control the governed; and in the next place, oblige it to control itself."

Got that? Men are not perfect, and when you give them power, the temptation to evil becomes overwhelming. So the government has to be held tightly under control, but it also has to be strong enough to do the tough jobs when necessary.

How do we do that? No one has ever managed it before. Here's the answer, according to Thomas Jefferson: "In questions of power, then, let no more be heard of confidence in man, but bind him down from mischief by the chains of the Constitution."

The Constitution is the key: a tightly written set of rules controlling those we elect to the central government. They have to obey the law, just like we do, and just do their job.

But we've gotten lazy. We forgot to stand guard. Now we let that government tell us what to eat, what to drive, how much we can earn, what light bulb we can use, how much water can be in our toilets, on and on and on. And it's common for over half of our income to be taken by government in various ways by many different taxes and fees.

The men who started America would call that "slavery." What do you call it?

It's time to stand up. You are a free man or woman, a free citizen in the most successful, generous, productive, and healthy country the world has ever seen. Act like it. Quit letting your hired servant run your life.

NO NEED TO SECEDE

The federal government, the thing we call "the United States of America," was created by us, working through our states. When we did it, each state (or "commonwealth," like Virginia) was completely sovereign. We no longer had to obey England, and had no other authority over us. Each state was an independent country, free to do what it pleased.

Then we agreed together to create a central government, the "federal" or "national" government, to do certain things. We did not give up our independence; we just hired someone to do a few things, and agreed that we would not do the things we hired them to do. Makes sense. One place to make the money we all use, one army to defend us all, that sort of thing.

In all things that were NOT assigned to the federal government, all the states were still independent and free. This may surprise you: they still are. You still are.

The goal was to create many "laboratories of freedom," fifty of them by now, with each state free to experiment with the balance between government control and personal freedom. If your state decided to make blue bicycles illegal, and you wanted a blue bicycle, you could just move to the next state. If they outlawed handguns, or abortion, or smoking, or eating salty popcorn, or praying in the schools, it would be a decision by the people living in that state, and everyone could then choose where they wanted to live and the kind of laws they wanted to live under.

But now the federal government has reached into every tiny corner of our lives and insists that we all "do it the same." Our freedom is disappearing. That's a problem, because now we are bowing down to a king again — we are enslaved to the whims and philosophy of whoever just got elected, or the radical opinions of the majority of the nearest federal court.

Besides being illegal, it's destructive. Here's why.

Everything the federal government touches that is outside its real authority takes away our freedom in the states to figure out how to do that thing more creatively and with better results. Whatever they touch gets more expensive and becomes controlled by political decisions, not smart decisions.

Look around you: the things that keep getting better and cheaper, and that make your life more comfortable and enjoyable, are the things done by people freely pursuing their dreams, not by the government. When the central government takes over, cost goes up, whether it's gasoline or healthcare or the schools, and things get worse, not better.

Before the federal government took over education, children were taught in homes or locally-controlled schools. Has education gotten better? Consider this example of an 8th grade test from Saline County, Kansas, from 1895:

http://www.salina.com/1895test/
(Reproduced in the Appendix as well)

Certainly that was a simpler time, before computers and space stations; but the exam shows a focus on real academic education across many subjects, unlike today's preoccupation with self-esteem and political correctness.

Today, home-schooled children score dramatically higher on standard tests than students in public (government) schools, even when the mom teaching them only has a high school education.

The federal government now tries to control major industries. Do things get better? People stand in line to buy the Apple iPad and iPhone, created by a company still free to invent things you want; but Chevy could not sell the government-sponsored Volt, even with tax credits stuffed into the glove compartment.

Washington has no business running schools or car companies; those things were not assigned to them.

In Texas we like to talk about our right to "secede" if we don't like what the federal government is doing. To secede would mean pulling out of the United States and becoming an independent country once again. Texas was its own country for several years before joining the United States, and there's a special pride and independence here about that. We love freedom, and the desire of Washington to run our lives just irritates and offends us.

But there's no need for any of us to secede. The law we live under gives us the right and all the power we need to correct the situation at hand; if we insist on making the federal government obey the law, everything will get sorted out and America can burst forth into full bloom again.

It's the opposite of seceding. We don't need to withdraw; we need to press in, to engage more aggressively, and force the central government to live by the law of the land.

What law? You can stick it in your back pocket, and still have room for your handkerchief and comb. It's called the Constitution, and nothing they do in Washington is legal unless it obeys what's in that short document.

The founders knew there was great danger that the national government would grab power and try to take over, abusing us and bullying the states we live in. Many of their predictions have come true. But they told us what to do if that happens and we can't get it under control.

If it gets bad enough, the answer is right there in the Declaration of Independence: *"Governments long established should not be changed for light and transient causes,"* but when a government stops protecting our rights, and goes beyond their *"just powers,"* then *"... it is the Right of the People to alter or to abolish it, and to institute new Government..."*

And even more, *"when a long train of abuses and usurpations"* occur, showing the clear intent of the government to control the people by *"absolute Despotism,"* then *"it is their right, it is their duty, to throw off such Government, and to provide new Guards for their future security."*

We are well into that "long train of abuses and usurpations" by the folks in Washington. We need to put an end to it.

As far as the right of the states to take action against these abuses, that idea was routinely in the air as they launched the United States as a new country. In 1798, James Madison, a primary author of the Constitution, wrote, "In case of a deliberate, palpable, and dangerous exercise of other powers, not granted by (the Constitution), the states who are parties thereto, have the right, and are in duty bound, to interpose for arresting the progress of the evil..."

Got that? "The evil." The states are "duty bound" to stop the central government from reaching into our lives illegally.

If we demand that the federal government get back within the lines drawn by the Constitution, and it refuses, then many states may try to pull away. We will either start over, or the greatness of America will collapse into a bankrupt, corrupt tyranny, filled with poverty and oppression just like so many other socialist regimes in the world.

Let's fix it, before it gets that bad! Let's get back to freedom.

Here's a quick review of the Constitution, which created and limits the federal government. It seems like dry stuff, but the result is amazing, the best government ever designed – strong enough to do the job, but strictly prevented from running your life – if this document is obeyed!

THE CONSTITUTION, IN ONE EASY LESSON

To better understand the Constitution, start with the Declaration of Independence. Think of it this way: the Declaration, in just a few words, spells out the ideas that will be the foundation and purpose for the new government, and the Constitution says how it will work. The Declaration explains "why," and the Constitution explains "how."

The Declaration explains what we are trying to achieve, and gives the reasons for doing it; it's like an architect designing a house. The Constitution is the detailed carpentry work to actually nail the boards together.

Many things are justified as being "constitutional" even though they are a slap in the face to crucial ideas set forth in the Declaration; by that, you know something is not right. As an example, consider this phrase: governments get "their just powers from the consent of the governed." When the federal government takes actions that are against the expressed will of the people, that is lawlessness. The will of the people is primarily expressed through the Congress that represents us, so when the President does something by executive order that the Congress has rejected or "refuses to do," he is trampling on "the consent of the governed."

Since we work through people we elect, the only time we can change things is at elections. That's good, because we can't rush into bad actions, but it also means there is plenty of time for damage to be done in the years between elections. The more we are controlled by agencies issuing regulations instead of by elected Congressmen issuing laws, the more our elections become meaningless. Agencies are not accountable to voters.

When our leaders despise the limits placed on them by the Constitution and use their freedom to pursue their own goals, that damage can be massive. That's where we are today, and we may not be able to recover unless we hurry.

All right. Let's look at the Constitution itself. Here's what it actually says. This won't take long; your coffee won't even get cold. If you don't have a copy of your own yet, read it at the Patriot Post:

http://patriotpost.us/document/the-constitution-of-the-united-states-of-america/

Ready? Let's walk through it.

The Preamble declares why the Constitution is being created. Since this is a preamble, a "whereas" clause, it has no legal power and does not authorize anything. But it gives a clear idea of what the founders wanted to accomplish. In fact, it's short and sweet, so let's print it here:

> *We the People of the United States, in Order to form a more perfect Union, establish Justice, insure domestic Tranquility, provide for the common defence, promote the general Welfare, and secure the Blessings of Liberty to ourselves and our Posterity, do ordain and establish this Constitution for the United States of America.*

(But the "Blessings of Liberty" are being stolen now, not secured. That's the issue.)

ARTICLE I sets up the legislature, which means the Congress, the group that writes the laws. It creates the House of Representatives and the Senate; gives them authority to do certain things; tells how Senators and Representatives can be removed when necessary; lists some things they are forbidden to do (like make someone king); and lists some things the states can no longer do, since the central government will now do them.

Pay attention to Section 8, which lists the things Congress has authority to do. Since it is so important, let's include it here:

The Congress shall have Power To lay and collect Taxes, Duties, Imposts and Excises, to pay the Debts and provide for the common Defence and general Welfare of the United States; but all Duties, Imposts and Excises shall be uniform throughout the United States;

To borrow Money on the credit of the United States;

To regulate Commerce with foreign Nations, and among the several States, and with the Indian Tribes;

To establish an uniform Rule of Naturalization, and uniform Laws on the subject of Bankruptcies throughout the United States;

To coin Money, regulate the Value thereof, and of foreign Coin, and fix the Standard of Weights and Measures;

To provide for the Punishment of counterfeiting the Securities and current Coin of the United States;

To establish Post Offices and post Roads;

To promote the Progress of Science and useful Arts, by securing for limited Times to Authors and Inventors the exclusive Right to their respective Writings and Discoveries;

To constitute Tribunals inferior to the supreme Court;

To define and punish Piracies and Felonies committed on the high Seas, and Offences against the Law of Nations;

To declare War, grant Letters of Marque and Reprisal, and make Rules concerning Captures on Land and Water;

To raise and support Armies, but no Appropriation of Money to that Use shall be for a longer Term than two Years;

To provide and maintain a Navy;

To make Rules for the Government and Regulation of the land and naval Forces;

To provide for calling forth the Militia to execute the Laws of the Union, suppress Insurrections and repel Invasions;

To provide for organizing, arming, and disciplining, the Militia, and for governing such Part of them as may be employed in the Service of the United States, reserving to the States respectively, the Appointment of the Officers, and the Authority of training the Militia according to the discipline prescribed by Congress;

To exercise exclusive Legislation in all Cases whatsoever, over such District (not exceeding ten Miles square) as may, by Cession of particular States, and the Acceptance of Congress, become the Seat of the Government of the United States, and to exercise like Authority over all Places purchased by the Consent of the Legislature of the State in which the Same shall be, for the Erection of Forts, Magazines, Arsenals, dock-Yards, and other needful Buildings;--And

To make all Laws which shall be necessary and proper for carrying into Execution the foregoing Powers, and all other Powers vested by this Constitution in the Government of the United States, or in any Department or Officer thereof.

That's it. That's the list of what they're allowed to do.

Some people think that two-thirds of what the federal government does today is NOT in this list, and therefore flatly illegal. And if something is illegal for Congress to do, then it is also illegal for the President to do, and illegal for the courts — including the Supreme Court — to be involved with. Just wait, we'll get into it.

Let's go on.

ARTICLE II establishes the executive part of the government, which means the President. It describes who can be President, how he will be elected, his oath of office, his responsibilities, and how he can be removed. (You know, of course, that "he" also means "he or she" in normal English.)

ARTICLE III creates the Supreme Court and allows Congress to create other courts. It describes the areas in which they would have jurisdiction (the right to make decisions). It also defines the crime of treason and discusses how it should be handled.

ARTICLE IV discusses the relationship among the states and the new federal government. It describes how new states can join the agreement, and requires the federal government to protect the states from invasion and domestic violence.

ARTICLE V explains what must be done when we want to change the Constitution, which has now happened 27 times.

ARTICLE VI says the new government will pay the debts of the prior government, and declares the Constitution, and laws or treaties made under its authority, will be the supreme law of the land (this is the "supremacy" clause). It further declares that all federal and state officials must take an oath to support this agreement.

ARTICLE VII says the Constitution would be official as soon as at least nine states agreed to it.

That's it. We've just described the entire Constitution.

But there were some significant additions to be made, and the Constitution would not have been signed without a commitment to get these done: so the first ten amendments are really part of what was agreed to when the Constitution was adopted.

AMENDMENTS: Next in your copy of the Constitution you'll see 27 formally adopted changes, including one that cancels a prior amendment. The first ten are called the "Bill of Rights;" these are the ones that many people required in order to agree to the Constitution.

Please understand that these are not a list of all of our rights; the whole Constitution, not just ten amendments, has to do with securing our rights as a free people, and our rights go far beyond the few things mentioned in this document. Some would say the only legitimate purpose of government is to protect our rights, and that's the only reason we put up with all the problems of having a government.

In fact, this is such a key idea, it will help you see clearly what people in Washington are doing. Pay attention. Are you ready? Don't miss this.

The Constitution does not give you any rights; it protects the rights you already have. You had them before the Constitution was written.

Did you get that?

You had the right to own weapons and protect yourself before the 2nd Amendment was written. You had the right to freedom of worship, and freedom from being arrested and searched without a reason. And so on. The Constitution simply prevents the federal government from taking any of those rights away, and insists they be protected — you already had them.

So if people talk about whether the Constitution "gives you the right" to do or say something, they have it backwards. Tell them, "No, it doesn't. And it doesn't have to!"

And if they tell you that you can't do something, because it's "unconstitutional," they've really got it wrong. The Constitution tells the federal government what THEY cannot do. If the courts have declared that you can't do something that you think should be your own decision, then you've probably found an example of the federal courts themselves violating the Constitution, trying to control a part of your life that is none of their business.

Seriously.

You'll hear all sorts of arguments from the news people and politicians about whether a person or a state can do something under the Constitution ... just listen for it. They typically want the federal government to control those things, so they want you and your state to NOT be allowed to do them. That's backwards.

And they (including some important elected officials) may have no idea what the Constitution actually says. It can be quite funny. And sad. And dangerous, because of the power they have to shape opinion and make law that controls your life. When many state and national elected leaders were asked about the constitutionality of the proposed healthcare bill in late 2010, their answers were often complete nonsense. These are people who had sworn an oath to uphold the Constitution, but they were clueless about what it says.

Remember: the Constitution was written to create and tightly control the new federal government, not to control you, and not to control the states. Can the state you live in pass healthcare laws, and electric light bulb laws, and motorcycle helmet laws, and too-much-salt-on-your-fries laws? Absolutely. Can the federal government do any of that under the Constitution? Not a bit of it.

Not legally, anyway!

FREEDOM. YOU CAN HANDLE IT. BUT HURRY!

A few parts of the Constitution have been ignored, others have been twisted, and increasingly we have a federal government that simply disregards it altogether.

Can you imagine that? Like a policeman walking around deciding which laws he'll enforce, and which he won't. "Sure, Sam, you can break into that store and steal whatever you want. I never did like that guy anyway. Just don't throw that aluminum can away, you know, recycling is important!"

For example, Article IV says *"The United States ... shall protect each of [the states] against invasion..."*

But large organized crime groups are currently coming across our southern border, invading several states to do so, and the federal government not only refuses to protect the states along that border, it brings lawsuits against the states that attempt to protect themselves. The primary lawyer for the United States announced that he had no intention of enforcing a recent law enacted by Congress. And as the first edition of this book was being written the President was aggressively implementing a wide-ranging, very controversial law that had already been ruled unconstitutional by a federal court.

So the increasing problem is a central government, created and controlled by the Constitution, that has no intention of obeying the Constitution at all. This is a new crisis. If it continues, it will bring an end to the United States faster than any of us can imagine.

Why?

Because if they don't have to obey the law, why do we? Why do you? Lawlessness by our national leaders encourages lawlessness by everyone else, and may even require us to break the law for our own self-protection. Several top members of a recent administration did not bother to pay their taxes until they were in office and forced to do so. If they didn't have to pay their taxes while they were private citizens, why do you have to pay yours?

And as we've seen everywhere else in the world, a corrupt government inspires corruption and lawlessness throughout society, which leads to the complete breakdown of the economy, public safety, etc. In places as different as Venezuela and England today, criminals attack anyone they want, and a policeman who tries to stop them can be punished as though he were the criminal. Their central governments have disarmed the citizens and become corrupt rulers who no longer protect the rights and safety of the people.

As this is being written, the Attorney General of the United States is simply ignoring the laws he does not like, and says so. His boss, the President, obviously supports him.

This is bad!

But in America, at least until recently, it's been more a matter of the federal government twisting the law than ignoring it, and different parts of the federal government do that routinely.

For example, Congress has the right to "regulate" commerce among the states. They say the "interstate commerce clause" means they can control everything you do, and everything you don't do, because whatever you do, or choose not to do, affects interstate commerce somehow, somewhere.

Does that make sense to you?

The meaning of the Constitution is being distorted on purpose. This is not a secret. But those who like government like power, and any reading of the Constitution that gives them more power is just fine.

Except the more power they take, the more freedom you lose. And you've lost a lot.

When a major law was passed at the end of 2010 which authorized the government to take over many of your decisions about doctors, hospitals, and health insurance, reporters asked the leader of the House of Representatives where in the Constitution she found authority to do that. Her answer was just to laugh, and say "Are you serious? Are you serious?"

They honestly believe they can do anything they want. And we have let them do it, to our shame. We have let the bully run the playground, and now he thinks he owns it.

Remember that the Constitution both creates and limits the federal government. If it no longer applies, and those in power do not have to carry out their assigned responsibilities nor stay within the limits of their assigned power, then the rest of it does not apply either.

Either it is the supreme law of the land, or it is not. If it is not, then the federal government itself does not legally exist, and everything those people are doing is illegal.

If it is the supreme law of the land, then they need to obey it just like you do. If the Constitution does not apply to everyone, then it applies to no one.

If it is no longer in effect, then the government it created no longer exists, and we are being told to sit down, shut up, and do what they say ... by people who no longer have the authority to say that.

What will we do then?

We need to require them to get back in line, before we have to answer that question.

FREEDOM. YOU CAN HANDLE IT. BUT HURRY!

THE SUPREME COURT IS NOT

Do you believe the Supreme Court gets to decide every issue, and we have to live by whatever they say?

So if they say your property will be taken away or restricted to protect the Gafoozle Butterfly or an "endangered" rodent, and suddenly your land loses half its value and you owe more money than it is worth, you're OK with that?

And if your state had laws against abortion, but the Supreme Court said those didn't matter? If they declared that doctors could just remove a baby from the womb anytime the mother wanted to get rid of it? Is that OK? No matter what your state, or the father, or the baby might want?

What if they don't really have that authority, and you are just letting nine unelected political friends of the past few Presidents put on black robes and run your life, when you don't have to?

The Supreme Court is not. Supreme, that is. You are. You, acting through your state.

Let's walk through this, because they probably did not teach you this in school.

And if you're new to this country, and you came here to get away from a corrupt, domineering government, you're going to be pleasantly surprised. You can help us avoid becoming a mess like the one you left. After all, if we don't fix this, and you have to flee America next ... where will you go? There is no place left. We are "the last, best hope," as President Reagan said.

So. Can't the Supreme Court tell us what we have to do, in every area of life?

Here's the key. Pay attention, this is crucial.

Yes, they can – remember that "supremacy" clause? – but only in the areas in which we have given them that authority, which is only in the areas specifically assigned to the federal government by ... ?

Right. By the Constitution.

Here's the key phrase:

> *"The judicial Power shall extend to all Cases, in Law and Equity, arising under this Constitution, the Laws of the United States, and Treaties made, or which shall be made, under their Authority ..."*

If the Congress passes a law that France must change the colors of their flag, what happens? If they pass a law that the moon must turn green, what happens?

They don't have the authority to do either of those things, so nothing happens, except that we might laugh. Neither France nor the moon are "under the Constitution" or "under their Authority," and therefore France and the moon are not bound by any laws Congress might pass.

But what if the Supreme Court hears the case, and decides, "Yes! France must change their flag!"

You tell me.

Right.

The important thing is to understand when the United States Supreme Court has the authority to make decisions... and when it does not.

Look again at the quote: "... *all Cases... under this Constitution, the Laws of the United States, and Treaties made ... under their Authority ...*"

So all we're talking about is laws and cases that are under the authority of the federal government as defined by the Constitution.

They do NOT have authority over everything else, any more than they have authority over the flag of France or the color of the moon.

Again, if the federal government does not have authority in some area, they don't have authority. Congress doesn't, the

President doesn't, and ... right ... the Supreme Court doesn't. We created the federal government to do certain things, and "no more," remember? There are many, many things that we did NOT authorize them to deal with – everything not on that list.

A related problem is our depending on the Supreme Court to protect us from abuse by the other parts of the federal government.

Here's an example of the Court's failure to protect us.

The federal government passed a very unpopular law requiring all of us to buy health insurance, or pay a penalty if we refuse. In 2011, more than half of the states sued the federal government to stop the enforcement of this law. In the spring of 2012, the Supreme Court heard arguments and began considering the matter.

The lawsuits said basically that the "interstate commerce" clause — remember that? — does not give Congress the authority to penalize us for NOT doing something. Seems obvious. But if you don't buy insurance, under this new law, you have to pay a penalty — for not buying a product they want you to buy.

 In the "oral arguments" part of the hearing, one of the judges asked the government attorney the obvious questions: if the government can require us to buy health insurance, then why not burial insurance, or broccoli? Is there any limit on what they can require us to do?

Obviously, the answer is "no." And when the Court upheld that law, they blew a gaping hole right through the Constitution.

Although bringing lawsuits was the obvious, necessary thing for the states to do, given how everyone thinks about the Supreme Court, there are disastrous problems with trusting in this approach.

The healthcare law is clearly unconstitutional, on the face of it. Go back to Article I, Section 8, and find the sentence where we gave Washington any authority at all over how we manage our healthcare.

I'll save you the trouble. It's not there.

The entire area of doctors, nurses, medicine, hospitals, insurance, etc, is a responsibility that belongs to us and to the states we live in. All meddling in that subject by Washington is flatly, completely illegal, whether the Supreme Court thinks so or not.

(Some might say they have that authority because of a "general welfare" clause. We'll cover that in a few minutes.)

Depending on the Supreme Court to reliably protect us from illegal actions by Congress is not our only solution, and these days, it can't even be our main protection. Since at least 1937, the Supreme Court has routinely failed in this task. Occasionally since then they have actually declared something Congress has done to be unacceptable, but normally they have supported the "progressive" idea that Congress has all the power it wants.

Another factor is that they only rule on the few cases that are brought to them. Our runaway Congress and federal agencies were already creating thousands of pages of new laws and rules each year, and recent elections ensured there will be an increased flood of new bureaucracy and regulation! The Court cannot deal with that. It could not keep up even if it wanted to.

Think of it this way. We hired a team to carry the mail, watch the borders, etc. That team included three brothers. Today, one of those brothers is demanding to know where you get all your money, what you pay your employees, how much water your toilet uses, what kind of light bulb you use, who you donate money to, whether you own a gun, etc, and he even demands that you let him manage your healthcare from now on.

So what are you going to do? Depend on one of the other brothers, a fellow who moves very slowly and only in a few situations, to stop him? And if that brother won't stop him, then it's OK, and you'll let the first brother run your life?

If you can't spell "tyranny," it's time to learn.

Obviously, the first brother is Congress, and the second

is the Supreme Court. Does that help you understand what's going on, and why suing the federal government in federal court cannot be the final answer? The law is wrong, whether the Supreme Court says so or not.

What is the role of the Supreme Court? It is just the highest court for the national government. That's all. It does what all courts do.

In the famous "Marbury v. Madison" case of 1803, the Supreme Court actively took up the role of reviewing federal laws to ensure they do not violate the Constitution. But we in the States clearly have that right and duty as well, since we are the ones who formed the central government and gave it a list of tasks ... and a list of limits, which it routinely violates today.

Today, we think the Supreme Court is the only group that gets to decide what is "constitutional" and what is not. But the founders encouraged everyone — the Congress, the courts, the people, the states — to decide for themselves, and to put up a serious fight when their authority or rights were violated. This balance, where each player in the game has certain authority and rights, only works if each player protects what belongs to him.

It's called "checks and balances." Keeping the government under control only works if no single part of the government takes over. If any of us don't defend what is ours, there is no "check" on the others. If we let the bully take over, all is lost.

If you're playing cards with three other people, and they get to change the rules whenever they want – but you don't – who wins?

Those founders would be embarrassed and infuriated that we have let this happen, after all the blood spilled and hard work spent to give us the best government ever invented.

As James Madison told Congress in 1789, "Nothing has yet been offered to invalidate the doctrine that the meaning of the Constitution may as well be ascertained by the Legislative as by the Judicial authority." In other words, "You guys in Congress have just as much right to decide what is Constitutional as the courts do!"

If you and Sam make an agreement, and Sam — only Sam — gets to decide whether one of you is cheating on the agreement, and what to do about it, what happens? Every time a problem comes up, it gets decided in Sam's favor. Every time.

Would you sign that agreement? Of course not. Neither did the founders of this country.

What's the right answer? You both decide if the agreement is being obeyed, all the time. It has to be that way. Or you go to a third party, an independent judge or jury, to decide between you.

So if we, the states, made an agreement among ourselves to create the federal government (to hire those three brothers), who gets to decide if someone is cheating?

We all do. We, taking action in each of our states, do, and they, the hired team, also do.

All sides have to stand up for their rights and responsibilities, and protect their authority when the other party crosses the line. Each has areas of responsibility and authority.

Actually we, the people and the states, have more — since, as President Reagan reminded us in his first inaugural address, we created them, not the other way around. The central government is a legal entity created by us, organized by us, and accountable to us for its actions.

And certainly we do not depend completely on one part of that organization to protect us from the other parts, especially in areas where they have no legal authority whatsoever!

Make sense? I hope so.

Is it confusing? Yes, because we have divided up the power of government and scattered it in various places – cities, counties, states, various parts of the national government – on purpose, so that no one person or group can take over and run your life.

Freedom is messy work, full of arguments. But here's the more important question: Is it better than tyranny? Is it better than living under a king who has total control of your life, and can put you in prison or execute you whenever he wants to?

I hope your answer is, "Yes!"

So. What's the answer to our first question, "Is the Supreme Court supreme?"

I think you know, now. Help others understand.

FREEDOM. YOU CAN HANDLE IT. BUT HURRY!

"GENERAL WELFARE" IS NOT ABOUT WELFARE

Here's a key phrase that is used to justify an amazing number of totally illegal actions, and to take money from you to pay for it:

> *"The Congress shall have Power To lay and collect Taxes, Duties, Imposts and Excises, to pay the Debts and provide for the common Defence and general Welfare of the United States; but all Duties, Imposts and Excises shall be uniform throughout the United States; ..."*

Well, there you go! Power to provide for the common Defence (as they spelled it) and general Welfare of the United States. That's their job, right?

Those who wish to control your life and take your money insist that means they can do anything that seems like a good idea, anything that sounds like it would be a nice thing to do for us. You know, look after our "general welfare."

So if they think our children are getting too fat, they can tell McDonald's what they can serve, and tell the schools what food has to be on the menu, and — it's happening today — whether you are even allowed to send a lunch to school for your kid.

If lots of people have high blood pressure, they can tell you to stop putting salt on your popcorn. And stop smoking. And stop doing things YOU like to do, as well as things you want other people to stop doing. Whatever they want. And send you to jail if you won't obey.

But doesn't the Constitution gives Congress the authority to do whatever it needs to do for the general welfare? And "general welfare" means lots of things — healthcare, keeping the environment clean, safety in our stores and factories, the price of housing, saving that Gafoozle Butterfly, whatever they can think of that's worth doing. Right?

Well ... no.

That's not what it meant to those who wrote it, and the only true way to read any law is to read what was meant by those who adopted it. (James Madison said so, and he was talking about this exact phrase, and exactly the way they are abusing it today.)

They are not responsible for your general or personal welfare. You are. Whether you eat the right foods, stay warm in cold weather, have a decent job, or get healthcare when you need it — that's your job, not theirs. Washington is not your mommy.

You have just walked into a very old conversation. There were huge arguments about this as the Constitution was being adopted.

If this phrase gave them a free pass to do whatever they thought was a good thing to do, the rest of the Constitution means nothing. The whole point of the Constitution was to create a strong but tightly controlled government that was only allowed to do a very few things, and those very few things were carefully listed.

As James Madison (the man some people call the "Father of the Constitution") said, "If Congress can do whatever in their discretion can be done by money, and will promote the General Welfare, the Government is no longer a limited one, possessing enumerated powers, but an indefinite one..."

He also wrote, "I cannot undertake to lay my finger on that article of the Constitution which granted a right to Congress of expending, on objects of benevolence, the money of their constituents..."

Translation: "If they can do whatever sounds like a good idea to them, they have become dictators with total, unlimited power. And I can't find the part of the Constitution that gives them any right to take your money and use it for charity."

Thomas Jefferson was more blunt: "It would reduce the whole (Constitution) to a single phrase, that of instituting a Congress with power to do whatever would be for the good of the United States; and as sole judges of the good or evil, it would be also a power to do whatever evil they please. Certainly, no such universal power was meant to be given them."

Got it? If they get to do anything they want for the "general welfare," they get to do anything they want, "good or evil." And we have become slaves, not free men and women.

There's more: notice where this phrase appears, and what the word "general" means.

The "general welfare" phrase we're looking at actually begins Article I, Section 8, the discussion about what Congress can tax us for. That Section is a list of the things we agree to give them money to do, and — pay attention — that's all they have the right to take our money for.

But they have the right to come after us with warrants and guns to get our money. Every dime the government spends is taken from someone, by force. The government has no money of its own. They either take from you by printing more money (which drains the value out of the money you already had), or they take it from you by force, as taxes and penalties.

So we have to control very tightly what they have the right to take money for, or they'll take everything you've got, say some pretty words, and give it to all their friends. (Sorry, it's true. Look up "stimulus bill" for a great example, and try to find out where billions of dollars went.)

All right, how do we correctly understand what the founders meant?

This section starts by saying they can gather taxes "to provide for the common Defence and the general Welfare of the United States..."

This sentence is not authorizing them, it is limiting them.

The items they are actually authorized to take our money for are in the list that follows. This opening sentence sets the stage by saying, "By the way, you can only do these things we're

45

about to list for two reasons (besides paying debt): defending everyone, and benefiting everyone."

The key is the word "general," meaning "everyone."

If they take our money and build a highway system across the country, that benefits everyone. That's a "general" benefit. But they can't legally take money from everyone and spend some of it to help just one city, or one business, or one state, and certainly not one person. That's an "individual" benefit, not a general one.

All those "individual" and local projects should be done by the states, by local charities, by regional agreements between states, etc. By you, if you want to. But the federal government, the central government, is specifically, firmly, carefully forbidden to do it. Anyone else can do it, but THEY cannot.

Here's an example that will show you how the people who wrote and adopted the Constitution understood this phrase.

In 1796, right after the Constitution was signed, a major fire destroyed much of Savannah, Georgia, including two-thirds of the homes in the city. It was a massive disaster. If it happened today, the President would be criticized for not having FEMA there ten minutes after the fire started. But what happened back then, when everyone was still involved who actually wrote and approved the Constitution?

Savannah asked for help from the federal government. It happens all the time now, after every flood, every hurricane, every disaster of any kind. But after much argument, the Congress said "No, that would be illegal."

Got it? They said, "No." And they were right.

Every state and every person in the country could send their money to Savannah. Every charity, every church, every social organization, every Congressman could send their own money to help. But the federal government, the "United States," was specifically forbidden from doing it by this word "general" and the list that follows. Forbidden. Because it's not their money to give away! It's yours, and it can only be taken and used for what's listed in Section 8.

Remember Madison's comment about "expending, on objects of benevolence, the money of their constituents..."?

So when Washington takes your tax money and gives part of it to an individual as a welfare payment, that is illegal. When they take your taxes and build a building in some distant city, that is illegal. They are taking money from you by force — at the point of a gun, remember, because you are absolutely required to pay your taxes — and giving it to a particular person, or town, or state, and that is forbidden.

It happens all the time. It needs to stop.

These little items are often called "earmarks," and they are added to every bill that Congress passes. In 2009 a huge "economic stimulus bill" was passed, and President Obama swore there would be no earmarks in it. Zero, none. So apparently the 6,000 or so earmarks in the bill slipped past him when he signed it.

Sure they did.

The real problem is that we like it. We like having our Congressman dip his bucket in the river of money flowing through Washington and do something special for us — for our state, for our city, or for us personally. So we vote for them again, and they do it again. And again, and again, and again.

Congressmen use earmarks to buy our votes. As long as it works, they'll keep doing it. We're addicted to the federal money, like pigs at the trough. As long as we keep being pigs, they'll keep stealing more and more money, making taxes higher and higher, and throwing more slop in the feed trough.

Let's stop.

Let's grow up. Let's stop stealing from each other, and give up our addiction to the flow of other people's money.

FREEDOM. YOU CAN HANDLE IT. BUT HURRY!

"INTERSTATE COMMERCE" MEANS ... WHAT?

In that same section we were just talking about, it says Congress can *"regulate Commerce ... among the several states..."*

Those in Washington claim that anything you do is under their control if it affects anything that might be sold from one state to another. And even if you decide NOT to do something, the fact that you are NOT doing it has an effect, so they can fine you for NOT doing it.

No kidding. Really. These are adults, if you can believe it.

Everything in your life can be traced back to some product that might have been shipped across a state line. The clothes you wear, the food you eat, the books and magazines you read, the television you watch, the radio, the Internet ... everything. So they use this phrase to justify taking control of absolutely anything they want to tax or control.

If you fall and break a leg, the plaster or fiberglass used to make your cast comes from somewhere. If the company that made it is in another state, well, there you go: interstate commerce! And if it was bought in your state, a supplier in another state lost that sale, so interstate commerce didn't happen. So interstate commerce was affected. There you go again!

That's how they get to make rules that control the doctor and the hospital. And you.

It really is that silly, and that obvious.

When Thomas Jefferson became President, he said, "A wise and frugal Government, which shall restrain men from injuring one another, shall leave them otherwise free to regulate their own pursuits of industry and improvement."

Can you think of a single area of your life in which that government leaves you free today to manage your own business?

But what did they really mean when they put in that bit about regulating "Commerce... among the states" in the Constitution?

The states were operating as independent nations, and as the country came together, each was trying to protect its income and particular industries. They started charging tariffs (taxes) on the products being sold from one state to another, and it became obvious that a mess was developing that would hurt everyone.

The essay called "Federalist 22" describes two problems: it declares that the various parts of the German Empire were taxing each other so aggressively that the European rivers had become almost useless for commerce; and it describes the problems other countries were having in doing business with our unpredictable collection of states. Clearly the new nation wanted to avoid those problems and get on with growing their economy (as we would say today).

So this phrase was inserted partly to allow the new federal government to address those problems.

It helps to realize that "regulate" may not mean today what it meant when they wrote the word; and remember, to understand any document — any law, any book, any comic strip — you need to know what the word meant to the person who wrote it, not what it might have come to mean later.

In Washington today "regulate" means to tightly control every detail of something. The many "regulatory agencies" in Washington are writing thousands of pages of rules every year controlling every detail of how every kind of business has to operate, and those rules are treated as though they have the power of law. (That's another problem.)

But when the founders approved the Constitution, they apparently used the word "regulate" to mean "make things regular" — to smooth things out, to remove barriers, to get roadblocks out of the way. To set things free to grow and prosper.

So by preventing states from charging tariffs at their borders, they made business transactions across state lines "regular" — normal, predictable, smooth. The goal was to enable the states to trade among themselves and grow, not to control every detail of everything they did and bury them in restrictions and rules.

Just the opposite of what they do today!

It would also help to understand that the word "Commerce" had a much smaller meaning then. As they debated the Constitution, those in favor of it assured everyone that the phrase would NOT give the federal government any control over manufacturing, over business inside the states, etc ... in fact, over most of what Washington tries to control today by using that clause! So "Commerce" meant the exchanges between the states and with other countries, not the manufacturing and building and selling of things within each state.

Today, we need to protect ourselves from the many ways the national government uses this clause (and others) to over-reach its boundaries. We need to establish a routine process in each state that lets us quickly reject federal "laws" that are actually illegal acts interfering with our local activities under a puffed-up interpretation of the commerce clause or any other part of the Constitution.

FREEDOM. YOU CAN HANDLE IT. BUT HURRY!

WHAT IS "NECESSARY AND PROPER"?

Now that you've seen how far they've stretched some of the phrases in the Constitution, you won't be surprised about another one.

At the end of the list of what Congress is allowed to do, it says they can *"... make all Laws necessary and proper for carrying into Execution the foregoing Powers..."*

You and I would take that as an obvious, simple thing. In fact, it almost wasn't included, because it was so obvious, but some founders were afraid they would have to pass laws about a bunch of tiny things if it weren't there.

Here's how it works.

If I'm going to dig a path and put in a concrete sidewalk, I'll need to buy a shovel and some gravel and cement, and I may need to hire some helpers. Those items are necessary and proper expenses in order for me to build that sidewalk. So I was given the authorization to buy a shovel, when I was told to build a sidewalk. It was included as a "necessary and proper" part of the task, without being spelled out in detail.

We have authorized Washington to take money from us to accomplish a specific list of tasks, including any additional "necessary and proper" expenditures supporting that list.

What do they really need in Washington for "carrying into Execution the foregoing Powers"? Anything beyond that short list is a distortion of the phrase, and beyond the legal limits of what they are authorized to do.

If you hear the phrase used to justify some action, carry it back to the list of things in Article I, Section 8, and see if it is really a "necessary and proper" item supporting anything on that list.

"STATES' RIGHTS" ... AREN'T THOSE GONE?

"States' rights" is a quick reference to all the rights that you and I still keep, after what was assigned to the federal government by the Constitution. As the Tenth Amendment says:

"The powers not delegated to the United States by the Constitution, nor prohibited by it to the States, are reserved to the States respectively, or to the people."

Those who believe the Constitution is a vague, mushy, ever-changing set of "guidelines" that change with the times, and that the federal government really should be in charge of everything, and believe all the stretching of the original phrases to cover everything in the world is just fine ... well, those people think there are no "states' rights" anymore, and that everyone just needs to do what Washington tells them to.

The sign in a recent Houston Natural Science Museum exhibit about Texas mentioned "states' rights," just in passing. Fortunately for all the uninformed schoolchildren walking by, the sign explained it meant that some people think "the states don't have to obey federal laws."

You can just hear the "pooh-pooh" comment from the teacher who brought the kids, and of course the children would agree. How silly to think you wouldn't have to obey the laws! Of course everyone has to obey the law.

Some people think that various court cases and amendments to the Constitution have basically done away with states' rights — that the Constitution has "evolved over time, don't you see, in this matter" — and the states must now follow the instructions of the federal government in just about everything.

Excuse me?

There are a couple of problems with that. A couple of enormous problems.

First, there is a process for changing the Constitution, and until that process happens, that little book that you should now be carrying in your back pocket is the law. Period. Ignoring it, as the courts may have done, does not change it. Pretending that it means something else does not change it. Assuming that all the court decisions between then and now have changed it ... no.

Many of the founders talked about this problem. They saw it coming.

George Washington said, "The Constitution which at any time exists, 'till changed by an explicit and authentic act of the whole People is sacredly obligatory upon all."

That is, either we change it, or we don't. And if we don't change it by the specific method adopted in the Constitution, then it still means exactly what they wrote. Period.

Secondly, this idea reveals a total misunderstanding of the Constitution.

What rights do we still have? What rights do the states have?

Here, I'll show you. It's not hard.

If you are an accountant, and I hire you to pay my bills, I agree not to pay them myself. It would be confusing, and silly, for both of us to do it. So I give up the "right" to pay my bills, while you're responsible for doing it. Make sense?

What "rights" do I still keep? Everything else.

Do you, my accountant, now get to tell me what car to drive, what doctor to choose, how much I can pay my employees, and whether I can drill in my pasture for oil?

Of course not.

You pay my bills, with the money I give you to do that. I decide everything else.

That's what "states' rights" means: EVERYTHING ELSE.

Everything else besides those few things we authorized Washington to do in the Constitution. Can you think of a few things that would be in the "everything else" list? How about healthcare programs? Manufacturing? Exploring for energy? Protecting our wildlife? How we run our schools, and what we teach our kids?

Much of what Washington spends our money on today is, in fact, outside its job description, and therefore illegal, and should not be legally binding on us. When they make us pay taxes to do all that, they are stealing our money to use it in ways we never said they could.

So why do we let them control us in so many ways?

Tell you what. Let's stop.

There are two basic steps we need to take. Both are very simple, and both are very hard.

First, we need to insist that the people we send to Washington shrink the federal government, instead of allowing it to grow even bigger. By the way, that means we need to stop letting them buy our votes by promising to give us things paid for by other people's money.

Secondly, we need to insist that each of our states stand up to the federal bully by declaring illegitimate federal actions will not be recognized in the state, and by empowering the county sheriffs to control (and even arrest) federal agents wherever necessary to enforce that.

You've heard the commercials. "This offer is void where prohibited." Pretty simple. Federal actions are void where prohibited, and anything not authorized by the Constitution (as it was adopted and amended) is hereby prohibited.

Nothing complicated about that! Any state legislature can deal with any federal action they consider illegitimate.

Will they make different decisions? Sure. So what?

Will it be confusing? Yes, as long as Washington keeps breaking the rules, stealing our money, and trampling our rights.

But will it keep us free?

Nothing else will.

FREEDOM. YOU CAN HANDLE IT. BUT HURRY!

ISN'T IT A "LIVING CONSTITUTION"?

You will hear this phrase from those who want an ever-increasing government to make everyone do ... well, whatever they want everyone to do. Recycle aluminum cans and plastic bottles, keep people from praying in public places, keep parents from spanking their children, prevent smoking, you know the list. They like the idea that the Constitution can be steadily reshaped into a document that the founders never intended.

And if you don't actually know what the Constitution says, they can make it sound good.

"Things change. The Constitution has to change with the times. It's old, you know. The issues have changed, things are different now. The people who wrote it did not know about airplanes, or computers, or the Internet, or cell phones. So the Constitution did not address those things. But here they are, and we have to deal with them, so we obviously have the authority to do so, and they would have put them in the document if they had known about them."

Actually, no.

Lots of things they certainly knew about are not mentioned. Plows, telescopes, false teeth, gardening, navigation instruments, mining, mathematics.

Good grief, the list is endless.

That idea reveals a total ignorance, maybe a deliberate ignorance, of the Constitution, and a desire to keep you ignorant. It also reveals an unspoken love of tyranny and a hatred of freedom — a willingness to have "them" decide everything for you, and an unwillingness to let you decide anything.

Those who promote the idea of a "living Constitution" forget or ignore why the Constitution even exists.

And they would not offer this argument in any other part of their lives, so it's obviously not a sincere opinion. Dr. Walter E. Williams asks if people who say it's a "living Constitution" would let the rules of poker be a "living" document, and let him change the rules as they play the game with him.

Of course not.

What about the contract and loan agreement you signed when you bought your house or your car? Can the bank change that every now and then, just to "change with the times" as the economy changes? No problem, right? They can change the amount of money you owe, or the interest rate you're paying them, whenever they want, without your permission, because, after all, the contract is a "living" document. True?

Nonsense. The document you signed is what matters, and what it says is the only thing that matters.

Remember what the Constitution was written for.

To control you?

No. To create and control the federal government.

You don't need the Constitution to give you the right to do anything. That's not what it does. You are a free citizen, not a "subject," and the government was created to serve you, not the other way around.

And since the Constitution specifically lists what they can do, and then says emphatically in the ninth and tenth amendments "that's all, no more, that's it," there is no need to list all the other things that are none of their business.

It did not mention all the modern inventions we use every day, and did not need to. If those inventions are needed by the federal government, they are covered under the "necessary and proper" phrase that authorizes the government to get everything they need to carry out their assigned job. We want them to have the newest weapons and communications gear, for example, to take care of "the common Defence."

But you, and the states, do not need constitutional authority to use all these things. Your rights do not depend on their being listed in the Constitution, and the Constitution is not somehow invalid because of things it does not mention.

The Constitution is a binding agreement. If it needs to be changed, it includes instructions on how those changes will be made. It is a very simple, clear document. Those who wrote it and voted on it argued over every word, and we have extensive records of what they thought and what they meant. It means what it says, and we know what it means.

To pretend anything else is not honest, and you would not allow any contract or set of rules to be changed that way, always being changed by the other party — and being changed in favor of the other party, every time.

And by the way, it is not an agreement between us and the federal government. They didn't sign it. The Constitution is an agreement among the citizens of the states, who then got their states to agree to it. It is the document which created, authorized, and limits what should be a small national government intended to do certain things for us.

We, the people, assigned governmental authority to various organizations when we created the state we live in and when we together created the federal government. None of them get to change their authorized duties on their own.

And certainly they don't get to seize authority in new areas just by saying, "Oh, you know, that's such an old document, things are different now. They didn't know about (choose your subject) back then, and people expect us to fix this!"

They work for us. They need some help remembering that. Anyone who can't read his job description, or doesn't agree with it, needs to be replaced. If their behavior is so bad we can't wait for the next election, impeachments and recall elections are always available.

As this edition of "Freedom" was going to press, we had the most lawless, reckless, and unaccountable government in the history of the country. The damage was already enormous, and indications of the impending financial collapse of the country were still being ignored by the party in control.

When will we say, "Enough"?

WHAT CAN WE DO?

What happens if you understand that some particular action of the federal government is actually illegal, and you decide to ignore it or disobey it?

Men with badges and guns come take you away, if it's serious enough, or if you resist long enough.

So, what can be done? What if all our efforts to elect better people, and our calls and letters and emails to our representatives, and all we can do, trying to fix Washington, does not turn it around?

The simple answer is that the states — my state of Texas, your state of Wherever You Live — have the right and the duty to stand up to this nonsense.

Does that mean the state pulls back out of the United States? Isn't that what started the Civil War?

No, it does not mean pulling out ("secession"), because the best solution is for the federal government to obey the law, not for the rest of us to give up and start over.

Based on centuries of tradition in English law (the foundation of our legal system in every state except Louisiana), the county Sheriff is the ultimate law enforcement authority in your life. Not the state. Not your governor, or the attorney general, or the highway patrolman with the flashing blue and red lights on the interstate highway. The county Sheriff. And he may not even realize it!

What does that mean?

If the federal bureaucracy issues a rule about something they actually have no authority to do — set limits on carbon emissions from a factory, for example — and a business, a factory, in your county is not obeying that rule, what happens? Let's say it's your business, your factory.

If you are violating a state law, then the state authorities need to deal with you. But what if you are obeying all the state rules, but you have somehow violated an unconstitutional rule written by a federal agency? In fact, there are so many agencies issuing so many rules, you are probably already breaking rules you've never heard of. If not, you will be soon!

When the federal agent comes to enforce the rule, he is enforcing a rule that is not valid. He has no authority, no jurisdiction over you in this matter. The flag of France, remember? The color of the moon?

I suggest that example just to point out that the Constitution does not give the federal government any authority to control manufacturing, to control factory emissions, or to "protect the environment" in any way whatsoever. All of that is the business of the states (and where regional solutions are needed, regional cooperation can take care of it).

How do we know? Because it is not in the Constitution. It is part of the "states' rights," the "everything else" that was not given to the central government. The matters *"reserved to the States respectively, or to the people."*

In addition to the areas not assigned to them, there are things the federal government is specifically forbidden to do. The states retained absolute control in these matters, attempting to prevent abuse of the citizens by the new government.

For example, the second amendment forbids the federal government from taking any control over your ownership of guns; as a free citizen in a free society, your right "to keep and bear arms shall not be infringed." The fourth amendment forbids them from searching you or your belongings without "probable cause" and warrants issued by the courts; your right to be secure "shall not be violated."

These restrictions are now violated daily by the federal government. "Shall not" gives them heartburn.

So the basic reality is that you are being attacked. You are being told to do something, and perhaps forced to do something, by an outside organization that has no legitimate authority to do so. You may be threatened with penalties, fines, even arrest, if you do not comply. They can close your business and bankrupt you, with no real authority to do any of that.

Your county Sheriff is the one you should call on for protection, just as you would for any other attack, any other violation of your rights or your property.

The Sheriffs need to understand the Constitution they have sworn to uphold, of course, and they may not have realized yet that their authority as the top elected law enforcement officer of the county includes the authority to deal with illegal federal actions there.

Although they already have the authority to act, many Sheriffs may need the active support of the state backing them up in order to confidently resist federal agents and withstand federal intimidation. Our legislatures need to clearly support the authority of county Sheriffs to say, "No, you don't!" when federal agents operate in unconstitutional ways in their counties.

So we have some work to do. Let's get started. You work in your state, and I'll work in mine.

Find the people in your state legislature who are working on getting the state to protect itself. If you need help finding them contact the Tenth Amendment Center (http://www. tenthamendmentcenter.com).

Help those representatives get elected and stay elected, and make sure your own representatives are supporting the effort.

Talk to your county Sheriff, and if he is not familiar with these ideas, get him in touch with the Constitutional Sheriffs and Peace Officers Association (http://www.cspoa.org).

There's a lot to do, a lot of resistance, and not much time left.

FREEDOM. YOU CAN HANDLE IT. BUT HURRY!

SO, HERE'S WHERE WE ARE

We are in desperate shape. One piece of the problem is that the federal government now has so much debt that just paying the interest on those loans will soon be impossible, and all roads lead to disaster after that. (See Mark Steyn's book "After America" for a detailed description of what's coming, and why.)

Even when we make major changes in the people we send to Washington, it seems impossible to stop our slide into financial collapse, or even slow it down. The 2012 elections in particular set the stage for tsunamis of new taxes, new debt, and new levels of irresponsibility.

When national bankruptcy happens, everything falls apart. You may have seen it, if you came here from any of several nations that have chased this dream called "socialism." Riots in the streets, police killing the protestors, dictators taking over. It's awful.

It's where we're headed, unless we can change course.

Have you seen rapid inflation, draining all the value out of whatever money you have left? Perhaps the joke came from Venezuela, but it could have been from many places:

Should you ride the bus or take a taxi?

Answer: take the bus. You have to pay when you step onto the bus, but you don't pay until you get out of the taxi, and the price will have gone up by the time you get where you're going.

Currency devaluations of a million to one have happened – which means your $10,000 would become a penny.

Our current national leaders are bankrupting the federal government – which means they are bankrupting you and me, because they have no money of their own – creating well over a hundred billion dollars in new debt each month, with no plan to pay a hundred trillion dollars of existing future commitments.

If those we send to Washington will not or cannot make the radical changes needed, only the states can really protect us.

All the states have to do is say "no" to Washington, and mean it. But they won't do that unless you and I demand it. "Going along" is far too easy, and saying "It's not that bad" or just remaining silent will be the automatic response from those who are not willing to make hard decisions.

No one wants to start over, when we have the best form of government ever devised, but Jefferson's opinion was that if we can't get the central government to behave, that time may come. May I remind you?

> *... That to secure these rights, Governments are instituted among Men, deriving their just powers from the consent of the governed, That whenever any Form of Government becomes destructive of these ends, it is the Right of the People to alter or to abolish it, and to institute new Government, laying its foundation on such principles and organizing its powers in such form, as to them shall seem most likely to effect their Safety and Happiness.*

We and the states can "alter or abolish" the federal government if it becomes necessary, and either replace it or return to being completely independent sovereign nations without delegating any of our authority or rights to a central organization. That's not "seceding." That's getting a strong, rebellious, disobedient and destructive servant under control.

Again, find out who represents you in your state capitol, and find out where they stand on this. Find out which state-level representatives and senators are already working on "nullifying" federal actions, and ask how you can help. Start talking to your county Sheriff about his role when federal agents try to enforce illegal federal actions. There are people speaking about this all over the country, so he can find out about it if he wants to.

This will be a new discussion for many. These are not new ideas, and they are only 'radical' to those who reject the basic ideas on which America was founded, but they are certainly not what we were taught in school! So be patient, as you 'hurry.'

On the other hand, the Constitutional violations by our federal government are increasingly aggressive and oppressive, so you will find many people actively working on resisting them. Join up.

If you determine that those who represent and protect you are not interested or serious about this, start working on electing someone who will be. Or run for office yourself. You don't have to be rich or smart or, thank goodness, a liar, to be elected to office. You just have to be old enough, and know what you want to get done, and be willing to do the work to get there.

FREEDOM. YOU CAN HANDLE IT. BUT HURRY!

DO YOUR HOMEWORK

You can see that these ideas are not new, the battle is not new, and the need to defend freedom never goes away. When you're ready to dig in, look at the suggestions on the following pages. These resources provide extensive background information, and are filled with footnotes, references, and even the actual historical documents. Everything we've covered is easily researched and confirmed. Fire up your Internet browser. Do your homework.

I particularly suggest Dr. Larry Arnn's book "The Founders' Key" as a great resource to understand what was going on with the writing of the Declaration of Independence and how that led to the way the Constitution was built.

For an excellent primer on what your Sheriff can do to protect us from unauthorized federal actions, go to Sheriff Mack's book, "The County Sheriff: America's Last Hope." To understand the ongoing battle between those who love liberty and those who love power and control, see Mark Levin's several books.

Call whoever represents you in your state capitol; find out how they will stand up against the increasing tide of federal abuses. You may find it difficult to get them to even talk with you, because they may never have read the Constitution they swore to uphold and defend, and they may think whatever Washington says is what they have to do.

Here's a good question to start with: "When the federal government does things that they are not authorized to do in the Constitution, or even things they are forbidden to do (like the TSA searching people without a warrant), what is this state going to do about it?"

If you don't get strong, clear, satisfactory answers, do what any good Texan would do -- raise some hell.

And hurry.

FREEDOM. YOU CAN HANDLE IT. BUT HURRY!

A FEW RESOURCES

The Declaration of Independence

http://patriotpost.us/document/the-declaration-of-independence/

The Constitution

http://patriotpost.us/document/the-constitution-of the-united-states-of-america/

The Federalist Papers and The Anti-Federalist Papers
(See Hillsdale College, "US Constitution: A Reader")

Hillsdale College:

"US Constitution: A Reader"
ISBN 978-0-916308-36-0
"The Founders' Key" by Dr. Larry P. Arnn
ISBN 978-1-59555-472-7
Online video courses on history and the Constitution
(http://constitution.hillsdale.edu/)

The Patriot Post:

"The Essential Liberty Guide"
Many historical documents
and many other resources
(http://patriotpost.us)

Mark Levin:

"Men in Black: How the Supreme Court is
Destroying America"
ISBN 1-59698-009-5
"Liberty and Tyranny: A Conservative Manifesto"
ISBN 978-1-4165-6285-6
"Ameritopia: The Unmaking of America"
ISBN 978-1-4391-7324-4

Sheriff Richard Mack:

"The County Sheriff: America's Last Hope"
**(http://sheriffmack.com/index.php/
constitutional-links)**
(http://www.sheriffmack.com)

Milton and Rose Friedman:

"Free to Choose"
ISBN 0-15-633460-7
(http://miltonfriedman.blogspot.com/)

The Tenth Amendment Center

(http://www.tenthamendmentcenter.com)

Matthew Spalding:

"We Still Hold These Truths"
ISBN 978-1-935191-67-4

Thomas E. Woods, Jr:

"Nullification: How to Resist Federal Tyranny
in the 21st Century"
ISBN 978-1-59698-149-2

NOTES

www.ingramcontent.com/pod-product-compliance
Lightning Source LLC
Chambersburg PA
CBHW031206020426
42333CB00013B/807